101
EVENTING TIPS

101
EVENTING TIPS
Essentials for Combined Training and Horse Trials

James C. Wofford

The Lyons Press
Guilford, Connecticut
An imprint of The Globe Pequot Press

To buy books in quantity for corporate use
or incentives, call **(800) 962–0973**
or e-mail **premiums@GlobePequot.com**.

The Lyons Press is an imprint of The Globe Pequot Press.

10 9 8 7 6 5 4 3 2 1

Printed in the United States of America

Designed by Sheryl P. Kober

ISBN-13: 978-1-59228-199-2
ISBN-10: 1-59228-199-0

Library of Congress Cataloging-in-Publication data is available on file.

Contents

Introduction

As you take up this sport of eventing, brace yourself—you are about to embark on a wonderful journey. This journey will take you to green, open fields that you and your horse can gallop across to your heart's content, over obstacles that you would never have thought of even approaching a short time ago, and to a complete understanding and trust in your horse that will border on the mystical.

Eventing is often referred to as the triathlon of the horse world. It is composed of three tests: dressage, cross country, and show jumping. At first glance, these tests may seem to work against each other. The physical fitness required for the cross-country test would increase your horse's tension, which would reduce your dressage scores, while the speed of cross country would make your horse difficult in the show jumping test. However, just the opposite is the case.

Once you begin to understand this sport, you start to see the horse not as a series of disconnected parts, but as a whole athlete, and a superbly trained one at that. Each of the three tests, if trained for properly, adds to the horse's education and well-being. For example, dressage improves your control of the horse, which in turn makes the show-jumping test easier. As your horse's fitness increases he becomes stronger, which enhances his dressage work. Because your dressage work improves, you are better able to canter to show-jumping obstacles in rhythm and balance, and thus your ability to gallop at cross-country obstacles at a higher rate of speed will grow.

This eventing journey will not just take you to a better understanding of your horse, but to a deeper understanding of yourself as well. Along the way you will find that you have become physically fitter and mentally more disciplined. Most event riders feel a responsibility to be as fit as their horse and to develop the same work ethic.

You may learn something about yourself when you have a bad day at the office, but still come to the barn and ride your horse at your scheduled time, maintaining your patience while you work through a training problem.

Once you start to compete, you will know the joy of feeling a horse that you have trained yourself jump effortlessly over an obstacle that you had been secretly worried about. There are few sensations equal to that of realizing that your horse now understands something you have worked for months to teach him.

Since most of this journey will take place in a country setting far from concrete and traffic, you will feel a connection with the natural world, which is a difficult thing to find in the twenty-first century.

You are about to start your journey now, and I wish you success and good luck. I hope this book helps you as you take your first few steps along the way.

I.

Getting Started

tip 1. Join Up

Join your local eventing organization. You can find a list of these groups on the United States Eventing Association Web site at www.useventing.com.

While you are at it, you should also join the United States Eventing Association (USEA). It is the national organization for eventing enthusiasts and will be an invaluable resource for you. The USEA has lists of grassroots organizations in your area, local coaches, dates of competitions close to you, seminars, clinics, and member activities.

tip 2. Look Before You Leap

Before you compete in an event yourself, go to a local event as a spectator. If you have been participating in other horse sports, you may be a bit confused by the relationship between the three phases of a typical event. One thing you will notice immediately is that events run according to a time schedule. The dressage and cross-country phases have very specific start times for each competitor, while the show-jumping phase is individually scheduled at some events, or simply run according to a posted division start time at other events.

A good trainer will attend competitions with you to prevent you from making mistakes due to nerves or lack of experience.

tip 3. Find a Trainer

Choose a good local trainer. You can find the names of nearby trainers on the USEA Web site. Do not necessarily hire the first one you find. You should develop a close working relationship with this person, so a little extra time spent on research will pay off later on.

Any good trainer is happy to have you audit his or her lessons. While you listen, ask yourself if the trainer seems patient with mistakes. You are going to make a lot of them while you learn to ride, and you do not need a trainer with a short fuse while you go through the process.

A good trainer can simplify things for you, and explain complicated concepts in an easy-to-understand manner. I think it helps to have a trainer who has ridden at a high level, but it is not completely necessary. Many high-level riders either cannot explain what you should do, or become frustrated when you do not immediately grasp the concept. There is a time and a place for a coach who is a "screamer," but not yet.

tip 4. **Curb Your Anxiety**

If you are prone to anxiety attacks when you are performing, get professional advice. Performance anxiety is a common condition, and there are plenty of resources that can help you get over this. Your trainer can probably suggest someone. In addition, you can often find listings in the phone book or through Google.

You should take the same attitude toward anxiety as you do toward needing to improve your dressage, for example: "Okay, I am strong over jumps, but I get nervous during the show-jumping phase. Due to my nerves, I do not ride as well as I do in my lessons, so I have to get help with my nerves." Before the phase you find difficult, sit somewhere quiet and make a video in your mind of how you are going to ride. From your lessons, you should have a fair idea of what to do to improve your performance. Rehearse in your mind what that sort of ride feels like. Then imagine how you should change your ride as your horse starts to misbehave. You have already made things better at home by changing how you ride; now mentally practice doing the same thing in the competition arena.

tip 5. Assess Your Strengths and Weaknesses

Once you understand eventing, make a written inventory of your own particular strengths and weaknesses as a rider. For example, if you have extensive experience as a hunter/jumper, you will not need much coaching for the show-jumping phase. However, you will need some expert advice for the dressage and cross-country phases. If you have a great deal of experience fox hunting, the cross-country phase will seem easy to you, but the dressage and show jumping may be strange new worlds. After you have developed this inventory, you will know which phases will need extra work in order for you and your horse to become proficient.

tip 6. Everything Is Everything

Do not be put off by the range of skills you need to develop in order to event safely and successfully. When you first study eventing, the three phases seem mutually exclusive. However, as your understanding increases, you will find that the various phases are all interrelated. For example, if you improve your horse's dressage, his show jumping will get better. If you get your horse into better physical condition, his dressage paces will become more athletic. If your horse becomes more confident in cross country, his dressage will become more forward. Once you think about eventing a little, you will see that each of the disciplines helps the other two.

tip 7. Finding a Horse

The horse you ride when you are getting started in eventing will be crucial to your enjoyment, so choose the right horse for you right now. You should already have made the list we discussed in Tip 5, and this will help narrow your search. For example, a good dressage rider can be successful with a horse who otherwise jumps well, but has never done a leg-yield. However, it is absolutely necessary that your prospect is a safe ride over fences. You will probably have to make some compromises along the way in terms of age, price, fancy movement, and so on, but you must refuse to compromise on your prospect's jumping technique and scope. As your skills develop, the time will come when you will be able to ride a wider range of horses, and you will start to be able to substitute your skill and knowledge for your horse's training, but if you are using this book to get started, that time is not yet.

tip 8. Just Say No

Don't buy a "project." Projects are for professionals. Don't buy a horse that runs away. Buy a horse that is easy to speed up, but more important, easy to slow down again. Don't buy a horse that needs an accurate ride to jump well, or refuses to jump at all. Accurate riding over jumps is for professionals. Don't buy a horse that kicks, bucks, rears, spins, or refuses to jump, or one who won't load in a trailer, won't stand quietly in the cross-ties, or won't ground-tie while he is being clipped or shod. Don't do it, even if he has a cute face, or is a grandson of Secretariat. Just say no.

tip 9. Try the Horse

Tip 8 covered the *don'ts* of buying a horse. What about some *dos*? Do ride your prospect, if at all possible. When you ride the horse, he should have a smooth, flowing walk, a rhythmical trot that is easy to sit, and a quiet, balanced canter. It will help if he already knows the movements that will be required at his competitive level. Make sure you try the horse over jumps at the height of the competitive level you are aiming for (i.e., 2'11" for Novice, 3'3" for Training, and so on). If you are aiming lower than Novice, it would be a plus if your prospect has successfully competed at a higher level. It will be a great source of comfort to you that your horse has already seen the problems that are new to you.

Do arrange to have a cross-country school, including jumping banks, ditches, and water obstacles suitable for your level. Your prospect's attitude should be calm and businesslike, both over show jumps and outdoors. If you have never jumped a natural obstacle, have your trainer jump the horse over the various obstacles that are available before you attempt to jump them, and start over the smallest possible obstacle before progressing to higher obstacles.

tip 10. Getting to Know Him

Once you have purchased a horse, learn about him. What is his appetite like? Does he like a big breakfast, or does he eat better at the evening feed? Does shipping put him off his feed? What about his legs? Be alert for any change in shape or temperature. You should get in the habit of checking all four legs at the same time every day, preferably at rest in his stall. Any unusual swelling or increased warmth is a warning sign, and should be taken seriously. Early detection is your best defense against soft-tissue injury. Study his competitive record if you can obtain it, and make a mental note of which disciplines are strong and which are weak. If he has never had a knockdown in the show-jumping phase, and you have some hunter/jumper experience, then you will not have to practice this phase as much as the other two.

tip 11. Are You Good to Go?

Lameness is a constant concern for the event-horse owner, so continuously evaluate your horse's condition and soundness. Once a week, have a friend jog your horse in hand, and watch carefully for signs of irregularity in his paces. If you cannot organize this, put your horse on a longe line and ask him to walk, trot, and canter briefly in both directions.

You are looking for any sign of limping, for sure, but also watch for any loss of action. Is he as free in his trot as he was last week? If you have started competing, did you compete on hard ground recently? Did he run away from you during your last conditioning canter, and do more work than you had planned? A horse does not have to limp to be lame. If he is equally sore on both sides, he may change the length of his step or stride, yet remain level. Knowing your horse intimately is the way to spot this condition.

Be a good horsewoman or horseman. Notice your horse's reactions when you ride him after you have longed him. If he is easier to ride after you have longed him for a few minutes, think about making that part of your training system. Many horses are better after they have gotten the kinks out, and that may be an easier process from the ground if you are still learning how to sit the trot.

Your vet is a valuable source of knowledge about your horse's care and conditioning.

Plan on having your horse's shoes reset on a regular schedule, and work the plan out with your farrier so that you arrive at competitions with your horse's feet in good condition.

tip 12. Regular Care

Your horse needs regular maintenance when it comes to worming, shoeing, and having his teeth floated. A good veterinarian is your best source of information about this, but your horse should have something to say about it as well. Some horses need to be reshod every four weeks, while others can go for six weeks before they need to have their shoes reset.

A young horse in competition should probably have his teeth floated every six months, while an older horse might be able to make do with annual checkups. Some horses seem to need monthly worming, yet others can thrive on semiannual tube worming. The rule is always to watch your horse. The old horseman's adage is that "the eye of the master fattens the mare."

tip 13. Follow the Rules

Learn the rules. There are about seventy-five different ways to get eliminated from an event, and not all of them involve refusals and falls. Don't be a statistic. For example, know the rules about circling on course during the cross-country or show-jumping tests. Is it okay? If so, when? Do the rules for cross country and show jumping say the same thing?

What about the rules on attire? They change for each of the three tests. Are spurs required? What about gloves? Can you carry a dressage whip into the competitive arena? What about a jumping whip? Make sure you know when it is legal to use a "gadget" bit, and when it is not. You can find the answers to all your questions at the United States Equestrian Federation's Web site at www.usef.org. In addition, the USEA provides rule updates in their quarterly member's magazine. If you don't know there is a rule about it, you are going to find out the hard way. Stay current about the rules.

tip 14. Ride, Ride, Ride

Ride as many different horses in as many different situations as you can. Eventing is a test of all-around horsemanship, so anything you can learn about horses, and how to ride them, will prove useful. If you can find the right situation, catch-ride for a local hunter/jumper trainer. You will get to jump a lot of fences on a wide variety of horses.

If your jumping skills are well developed, gallop racehorses. Usually you can gallop four horses in two hours, and most race trainers like event riders because they have better hands than the average exercise rider and are more patient with young horses. You will be amazed at how fit you get when galloping, which will help your eventing immeasurably. The extra money helps, too.

The FEI Horseman of the Century, Mark Todd, is famous for having won the eventing Individual Gold Medal in two Olympics. What is less well known is that he also rode in the Olympics in grand prix show jumping, and competed successfully in steeplechase races. He is currently a flat horse trainer in New Zealand, where he is one of the leading trainers. Not a bad record to emulate.

In addition to reading as much as possible, never pass up the chance to watch other riders. Even if you are not participating, audit clinics and lessons.

tip 15. Reading and Riding

You can't learn to ride from a book, but reading books will certainly help you while you learn how to ride. The bibliography in the back of this book will help you get started. Don't try to read all the books at once. Read one every six months, and take some time to practice the new techniques that you have picked up. Many of the books on this list have been written so that you can go to them with a specific problem in mind and easily find a suggested solution.

The Chronicle of the Horse is published weekly and is the go-to source for competitive news. *Practical Horseman* is published monthly and has good how-to articles that will keep you up to date on every aspect of riding and horse care. The USEF and the USEA both publish magazines, and they are a good source of information about eventing and horse sports in general.

tip 16. Plan Ahead

You will usually know well in advance what the order of the three tests will be, and you should plan accordingly. For example, some competitions follow dressage with show jumping, while others have cross country follow dressage, and show jumping is the final test. A competition that takes place over more than one day will require a lot more changes of competitive attire than one that takes place on one day. As soon as you can find out your start times for the dressage, cross-country, and show-jumping tests, make out a time schedule for yourself. Are you going to ship your horse to the event the day before, or early that morning? The decision you make obviously affects what time you should set your alarm clock.

Decide how much time you will need to get your horse clean, tacked up, and ready for your dressage test. Know when the show-jumping course will be ready for walking at your level, and plan a time when you will walk it. Make sure you walk the cross-country and show-jumping courses for your level. Some competitions use the same general track for all the levels, and other competitions change the track of the course for each level. Go through the same planning process for each of the three tests. You should know where you are going to be throughout each day of the competition, so that you use your time efficiently.

tip 17. Saddlery

Make sure your saddle fits your horse. Nothing except bad shoeing or barbed wire will make your horse lame faster than a saddle that does not fit. Your local tack shop will be able to advise you, and many times saddle manufacturers give free saddle-fitting clinics. Once you are sure the saddle fits your horse, make sure it is suitable for you as well. When you are getting started in eventing, you don't really need a saddle for each discipline. A comfortable all-purpose saddle is fine for now.

Most tack shops have a used-saddle section, and if you are willing to shop around, you can usually find good-quality saddles in usable condition for a substantial discount from the original price. The used-saddle section is a good place to start, as your tastes will change as you gain experience. The only thing you can be sure of is that your first saddle will not be your last.

As you progress up the levels, you will eventually want a saddle for each phase. I recommend that you get a dressage saddle next, and keep your all-purpose saddle for cross country and show jumping. Good dressage and show-jumping saddles are easy to find, but when you eventually shop for a cross-country saddle, remember that the reason you are buying one is to be able to ride with shorter stirrups due to the increased speed of the upper levels. Make sure the flaps are cut far enough forward and that the balance point of the seat is farther back, so that you are comfortable with shorter stirrups.

tip 18. Fitting the Jumping Saddle

How can you tell if a jumping saddle fits you? (Remember, it is a given that it fits the horse—that always comes first.) Sit in the jumping saddle, and move around until your seat bones find the low spot in the saddle. Saddlemakers call this point the *swale*, while I call it the *balance point*. Whatever you call it, your seat bones should be able to find it easily. Then have your coach or a friend lift your heel up until you have a 90-degree angle behind your knee. Now look down at your knee. If you have the feeling that the saddle is formed around your knee, then the saddle fits you. If you have the feeling that the knee roll is under or even behind your knee, then the saddle is too short for you. Most saddles are built too straight these days, but occasionally you may have the feeling that there is too much saddle in front of your leg, in which case the saddle is too long for you.

This rider has outgrown her saddle. Her knee is beyond the knee roll, which will cause her to slip her leg back in the air over jumps, and to topple forward when she lands.

tip 19. Saddle Pads

Purchase a saddle pad at the same time you purchase your saddle, to make sure you have a pad that fits and is the right shape for your saddle. Basically, you want a square pad for dressage and a shaped pad for the jumping phases. In both instances, the pad should extend only one inch below the flap, in front of the pommel, or behind the cantle in any direction. Artificial fleece is acceptable, and much easier to maintain than natural fleece. Your horse is not a billboard, so do not adorn him with the name of your local tack shop, or any popular slogan. "Eventers do it three ways in three days" is funny, but not on your saddle pad.

tip 20. Nosebands

You are allowed four basic types of noseband for the dressage test: cavesson, figure-eight, flash, and dropped. The simplest is the cavesson, which should be fitted so that there are two fingers' width between the bottom of your horse's cheekbone and the top of the cavesson. Adjust the tightness so that you can just place one finger under the noseband.

The figure-eight is for horses that resist by crossing as well as fixing their jaws. The figure-eight should be adjusted so that the top strap fits below your horse's cheekbone, the two straps are at the same angle to your horse's jaw, and you can fit one finger under the lower strap. Purchase a figure-eight with a sliding piece on the top of the nose, as a figure-eight with a fixed cross-piece is very difficult to adjust correctly.

The flash noseband is very fashionable right now, but is actually an inefficient figure-eight. If the cavesson part is fitted correctly, the flash attachment is at too high an angle, and if the attachment is adjusted properly, the cavesson is pulled down your horse's nose. If your horse crosses his jaw and needs some correction, use a figure-eight instead of a flash.

Dropped nosebands are useful when you need to keep the attention of a horse with a "busy" mouth. Like a figure-eight, a dropped noseband is difficult to fit correctly unless it has an adjustable nose piece. Be careful not to make it too tight, as it can press on the soft cartilage of your horse's nose and restrict his breathing. As with the other nosebands, you should be able to slip one finger under it.

Do not base your choice of noseband on what the leading rider of the year is using. Study your horse, watch his reactions to the use of the rein aids, and then decide.

Regardless of your choice of noseband, try to train your horse on a daily basis with a simple cavesson. The more complicated nosebands are very similar in action to gadget bits. They work very well at first, but your horse soon figures out how to avoid the action of the gadget, and you are back where you started. Train your horse, don't trick him.

tip 21. No-Bling Zone

Eventing requires three different sets of equipment for the three different tests. When you purchase your equipment, remember that it is about the horse—it is not about you. By this I mean that your equipment should be of the best quality you can afford, but do not buy your tack based on the latest fad. The leather in your bridle should be flat, of an appropriate width for your horse's head, and devoid of all ornamentation. Make sure your horse is a "no-bling" zone.

Your reins should be an appropriate width for your hands, but not raised or swelled. Rubber reins are useful for jumping, and should be black or dark brown, not an unnatural color. Web reins are for riding in the rain, not for everyday use. The leather stops on the reins will invariably make your reins too short or too long.

This rider radiates confidence and preparation. Her horse sparkles and her tack is clean and correctly adjusted, although I would recommend a fitted saddle pad for jumping, not a square pad.

tip 22. No Rules, Just Right

There are rules regarding the equipment you are allowed to use before and during the competition. These are commonly referred to as the "no gadgets" rules. You are also required to wear a helmet while you are on the competition grounds. While there are no attire regulations for the warm-up before the competition, you should still be guided by good taste and judgment. Chances are you are not going to meet Mr. or Miss Right in the warm-up, so dress accordingly. Plus, if you are doing your job at the competition, you will not have time for Mr. or Miss Right-Now because you will be too busy.

Although you are not being judged during the warm-up, judges are human. If they catch a glimpse of you riding around looking like an unmade bed, I can guarantee you it will show up in your score. Onlookers should say to themselves, "Wow, look at the sparkle on that horse's coat!" They should not say, "Ugh, look at the Britney wannabe, with the bare midriff and muffin tops!" There is a world of difference between taking pride in your appearance and making a spectacle of yourself.

If need be, get a significant other to groom for you. This has its hazards, but they already know you are horse-crazy, and if they can't deal with that, they will not remain significant.

tip 23. Here Comes the Groom

Get someone to help you during the event. Grooms might seem like a luxury, but they are more like a necessity. An extra pair of hands can allow you to maximize your time. It is nice to finish walking the cross-country course late in the afternoon and come back to a horse that has been groomed, fed, and put to bed. Your trainer may be able to help you find someone to fill this role. If hiring a groom is beyond your budget, find someone you can trade places with. He or she can groom while you compete on one weekend, and then you can groom for him or her the following weekend.

tip 24. Bit by Bit

Once your horse is perfectly trained, he should compete in a plain snaffle bit and simple cavesson noseband. However, you have a great deal of work to do between now and then, so you need to know a little about specialty bits. The bits you are allowed to use during the dressage test can be found on the USEF Web site, www.usef.org. The

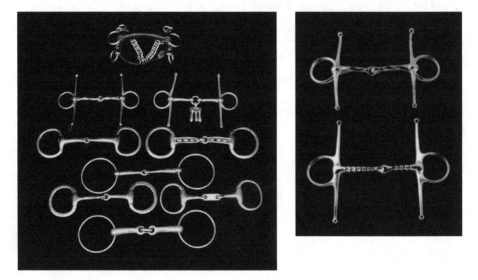

The bits shown here are typical of the bits that I use daily. Not all of them are legal for the dressage test, so make sure you check before you attempt to use them in competition.
Photo credit: Brant Gamma

choice of bits during the cross-country and show-jumping tests is left up to you, so you have a greater variety of bits to choose from.

If you have control issues over fences, go through a quick mental checklist. Horses pull in three different ways: down, up, or straight out. Determine which way your horse pulls before choosing a bit.

For example, if your horse pulls out and down, he needs a bit with a gag action. In this case, I prefer an American gag. The action of this bit lifts your horse's head and neck up and back. If your horse elevates his head and neck while he pulls, you need a bit with some form of curb chain. In this instance, I usually recommend a Pelham with a single-rein adapter. The curb chain action tends to round your horse's neck, which will help you to control him. Finally, if your horse pulls straight out, you need a bit with a corrugated surface, such as a slow twist or a corkscrew snaffle. Horses tend to "back off" of a bit with a corrugated surface, which is what you want if your horse is leaning out on the bit too much.

tip 25. Save the Gadget

Once you find a bit that helps you control your horse, try not to use it too often. If you use a gadget bit every time, your horse will soon find a way to ignore it, and you will be back where you started. Train your horse correctly in simple equipment at home, and save the gadget bits for the competition. If your dressage work is correct, eventually you will not need any tricks or gadgets.

Gadget bits can give you a gratifying improvement in your ability to control your horse. However, this effect is short-lived and will soon disappear, leaving you with a horse that has been controlled through pain rather than through education. Once you run out of gadget bits, you will be unable to control your horse, and you will have to go back to square one and start over. It is a funny thing about riders—they always have time to do it over, but they never have enough time to do it right in the first place.

tip 26. Feeling Good

You will get an enormous sense of satisfaction from feeling that you and your horse are improving. Bert de Nemethy, the legendary coach of the U.S. Equestrian Team, said, "A good feeling after the round is better than any ribbon." Focus on this feeling, and not on your short-term results. You and your horse will be the better for it in the long run.

At the same time, you need to learn *how* to get better in order to get better. You will need endless lessons in each of the three disciplines, you will need to watch videos, take clinics, study photographs, read books and magazines, and ceaselessly try to gain more information about your sport. But in the final analysis, *you* are the one who is going to have to improve, so remember this: Find out what you are doing wrong, and stop doing it! Practice doesn't make perfect. Perfect practice makes perfect.

Dressage

tip 27. Listen to Your Horse

You are going to have to take a great deal of dressage instruction while you learn how to ride and event. You will be exposed to various systems of training, and much of the advice and instruction you get will seem contradictory and confusing. This is part of the process, and you just have to work through it. As you develop your skills and knowledge, you will start to be attracted toward one type of horse, and one trainer's advice will make more sense to you than another trainer's. Again, this is part of the process, so settle down and enjoy it.

However, as you learn about your horse and about eventing, keep one simple adage in mind: Any system of equitation that disturbs the tranquility of the horse is flawed. If your horse is not learning in a calm, disciplined fashion, you must lower your demands on him. It is hard to teach anything except the wrong thing to an excited horse. Once he relaxes he will comprehend what you are trying to teach him and you will then be able to make progress.

tip 28. Dressage Attire

When you present yourself for the dressage test, the dressage judge is going to form an immediate impression of you, so make it a good one. The overall picture should be of impeccable turnout and understated elegance. A plain, three-button show coat in dark navy or black, tan britches, dark gloves, black dress boots, black spur straps, simple Prince of Wales spurs, and a USEF-approved helmet are all you will need to make the right impression. It goes without saying that your boots and spurs sparkle, and your coat and britches are just back from the cleaners.

A lady should wear a hairnet if her hair falls below her collar, and a gentleman with facial hair should make sure he has seen his barber recently.

A horse and rider turned out correctly for a Novice level event. I like the understated elegance of this photo, and would only add that even at the Novice level, I want the horse's mane braided.

Photo credit: Stacey Nedrow-Wigmore/*Practical Horseman*

tip 29. Ride Without Stirrups

If you want to ride dressage well, you must develop an excellent dressage position. This takes time, and a great deal of hard work, but the results are so beneficial that you will be pleased with the results. Make a habit of riding without stirrups. This is one of the best exercises available to improve your seat. If your local trainer is willing to help you, a series of longe lessons without reins or stirrups will help you improve your position remarkably. Start out riding without stirrups at the walk. Just keep them crossed over the front of the saddle, walk around for a few minutes, regain your stirrups, and start your dressage session with your stirrups. Gradually increase the length of time you can ride without stirrups, and start to ride without stirrups at the trot and the canter as well. (Practice at the canter before the trot—it is more comfortable, and it will increase your confidence.)

As a safety measure, do all of the above work in an enclosed arena at first. Once your confidence and fitness improve, try the same exercises outside. Make sure the terrain is more or less level. Sitting the trot without stirrups downhill is not for people who are just developing their dressage position. If you are going to do some dressage work without stirrups and then go for a hack, regain your stirrups and shorten them one hole. This will improve your stability in case your horse misbehaves.

If you can take an entire dressage lesson without stirrups and not think about it until you are done at the end of the lesson, then you have a good position, and your dressage work will reflect it.

This rider has a good stirrup length for riding dressage through the Preliminary level. Later on, I would like to see the stirrup leathers one or two holes longer, and the legs an inch or so farther back behind the girth.

tip 30. Dressage Stirrup Length

To determine the correct stirrup length for dressage, halt your horse and take both feet out of the stirrups. Adjust your stirrups so that the tread of the stirrup is two holes below your ankle bone. Replace your feet in the stirrups with the balls of your feet on or just behind the center of the tread of the stirrup. Your heels should be down lower than your toes, although not as deep as for jumping. This will provide a good depth of seat for dressage. Later on you will need to ride with longer stirrups, but right now you should sacrifice sensitivity for stability.

tip 31. The Dressage Position

Think of your dressage position as two straight lines: one line runs down from your ear to your shoulder, then through your hip to your heel; the other one is a straight line from your elbow to your horse's mouth. Let your weight settle equally on your two seat bones and your pubic bone. Lift your chest up and allow a small arch to form in the small of your back. This arch is important because it allows you to follow your horse's movement without gripping. If your back becomes flat or rounded to the rear, you will have to grip with your thighs and knees, which will make you stiff.

Let your legs hang naturally, and keep your feet at the same angle to your horse's sides as the angle with which you walk. At all times you should attempt to maintain a natural position in the saddle. If your instructor tells you to turn your feet parallel to your horse, leave your feet and ankles relaxed and turn your entire thigh instead. This motion puts the flat of your thighs against the saddle rather than the rounded part, and opens up the inner pelvic area so that you can sit closer to your horse.

tip 32. Hands and Arms

Carry your elbows close to your sides, and put your thumbs on top of the reins as they come over your index finger. Keep a little pressure on the reins with your thumbs to help prevent your reins from getting too long. Turn your thumbs just to the inside of a vertical line, and make sure there is no bend in your wrists. A straight line should go through your wrists to the horse's mouth. As a quick check of the straight line between your elbow and your horse's mouth, make an imaginary toy pistol with your hand. If your reins are adjusted correctly, your index finger will be pointing at the corner of your horse's mouth.

tip 33. Good Hands

Your dressage position is important because a good position allows you to effortlessly follow the motion of your horse. You will not be able to communicate with your horse efficiently until you achieve this position, and you will not be able to have "good" hands, much less "trained" hands. Good hands take when the horse gives, and give when the horse takes. Trained hands take when the horse takes, and give when the horse gives. Dedicate yourself to developing a classically correct position; your horses will thank you for it, and the dressage judges will reward you for it.

tip 34. The Leg Aids

There are three main leg aids: both legs at the girth, one leg at the girth, and one leg behind the girth. Both legs at the girth tell your horse to go forward. One leg at the girth asks for impulsion or bending. One leg behind the girth is to control or displace the hindquarters. Naturally, there

This rider has applied the first leg aid at the girth without displacing her leg. If the second leg aid is applied correctly, you cannot tell the difference between the first two aids unless you are standing in front of the horse.

are an infinite number of combinations of the aids, but think of them in this way and learn to use one leg independently of the other. For example, using your outside leg to ask your horse to canter does not mean you should be gripping with your inside leg and crumpling over to the inside.

Be very clear and very consistent in the use of your leg aids. Say the same thing each time in a clear way to your horse, and then insist on the same answer.

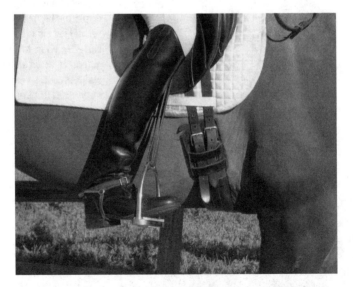

The third leg aid is usually applied about six inches behind the girth.

tip 35. The Goldilocks Leg: Just Right

The most important thing your horse can learn is to respond to your leg aid. Unfortunately, not all horses are born knowing how to do this, so you have to develop different ways of teaching different horses what the leg aid means. Some horses, especially Thorough-breds, are overly sensitive to your leg, and explode at the slightest touch. They must be taught to accept your leg, usually by means of a great amount of lateral work such as turns on the forehand and leg-yielding. Nervous, agitated horses with an exaggerated response to your leg do not thrive under a training system that emphasizes "Keep your leg on, keep your leg on, drive, drive." Horses of this type need a soft, consistent leg, often without spurs at first. A "hot" horse will try to teach you to take your leg away from his sides, but you should not buy into this; he must wear your leg like a second skin.

Horses that are "dead to the leg" should be ridden with spurs and a dressage whip. Each time you want to make a transition up to the next pace, you must be prepared to sharply remind your horse that when you close both legs at the girth, he must *immediately* move forward. The sequence of aids should be legs, spur, and then whip, all close together. Your horse must learn that if he does not move forward from a subtle leg aid, a sharp leg aid will follow. This is a very good time to make sure you have an independent position in the saddle. It is a natural reaction to tighten your hands when you tighten your legs, but you should not do this.

Horses will always listen to the aid you did not want them to hear. The hot horse will flee from the slightest motion of your leg, no matter how firm your hand. The lazy horse will stall from the subtlest twitch of your hand, even though you are kicking like crazy. Make sure your aids are extremely clear to your horse.

tip 36. Keep the Horse in Front of Your Leg

One of the most common forms of resistance by your horse is to ignore your leg aids. If this occurs, a gentle tap behind your leg with your dressage whip will go a long way toward improving your horse's attitude. One of the few universal truths about training horses is that your efforts are doomed to failure unless your horse is "in front of your leg." This means that your horse responds to the slightest pressure of your leg aid by moving forward. If you do not have this response, everything else will be wrong.

Now that you know this, you can easily recognize that your horse must be in front of your leg at all times. If your horse starts to fall behind your leg, use your spur. If that does not work, immediately apply your dressage whip behind your leg.

tip 37. Speak Softly, but Carry a Big Stick

Horses that are normal to sluggish in their reactions to your leg aids should be ridden with a dressage whip. You won't have to carry a whip on a hot horse for quite a long time in his training. Learn to carry your whip equally well in either hand. The only way you will be able to do this is to practice with your whip in either hand. Once you become comfortable with this, you can start to carry the whip on your horse's stiff side.

Carry the whip so that your hand and arm remain in a correct and natural position. You do not need to hold the whip in a death grip with all five fingers. If you let it, the whip will stay comfortably in the curve of your thumb and index finger. Practice changing the whip from one hand to the other without upsetting your horse. You can either put both reins in your whip hand and draw the whip up through your whip hand onto the new side, or put both reins in your whip hand and reach over with your other hand and roll the whip onto the new side. Whichever way you choose to change your whip, make sure you can do it without disturbing your horse.

tip 38. The Rein Aids

There are five rein aids: direct rein, open rein, neck rein, indirect rein in front of the withers, and indirect rein behind the withers. The direct rein is used to help control your speed and direction. If you squeeze both reins equally, your horse should slow down. If you squeeze one hand, your horse should turn in that direction. An open rein is when you move your inside hand away from your horse's neck without changing the pressure on the rein. The neck rein is when you bring your rein against your horse's neck at the withers. The open rein and the neck rein work best when they are used in harmony.

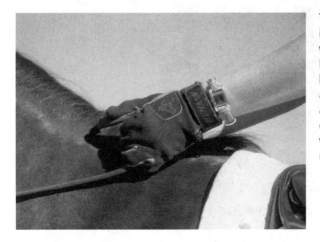

The direct rein feels as if you are squeezing water out of a sponge. In this photo, the rider's hand has turned slightly as she applies the direct aid. Practice until you can squeeze the sponge without pulling on the rein.

The open rein comes away from the neck, but the contact does not change. (Remember, the open rein does not work very well unless you are closing the opposite leg at the same time.)

The neck rein presses against the withers, and is usually applied together with the leg on the same side. The hand and wrist should not change shape as you use the neck rein.

The indirect reins are tricky to use because they act across your horse's body as well as directly through your horse. The indirect rein in front of the withers is mainly used to straighten a horse with a

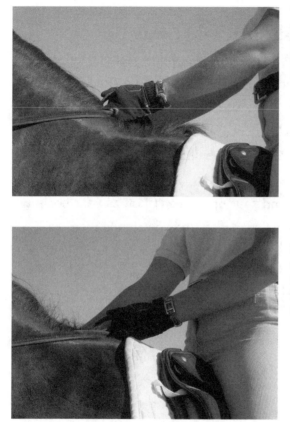

The indirect rein in front of the withers is used to change the angle of your horse's head if he is tipping it during his dressage work.

The indirect rein behind the withers is used in coordination with the direct rein as a strong turning aid. Both of the indirect reins cross the withers.

crooked head or neck carriage. The indirect rein behind the withers is a powerful turning aid when used in coordination with direct rein on the opposite side.

tip 39. Sit Still and Shut Up

Once you apply an aid, make sure your horse responds to it. If you close your legs, your horse must smoothly, energetically, and *immediately* move forward. If you squeeze your hands on the reins, he must slow down. However, once you have applied an aid, it is your horse's job to respond. By this I mean that if you put your legs on and your horse moves forward, cease acting with your leg. If you get what you asked for, sit still and shut up. It won't last, as your horse will soon either speed up or slow down, and you should then make the appropriate correction. If your horse is well trained, he will not need constant support and correction. Teach him what you want, ask him to do it, then sit quietly while he does it.

tip 40. Know Your Stuff

Know your dressage test. Your horse should not practice the test too often, as he will soon start to show off and "anticipate" the movements. Practice short segments and vary the order you practice them in so that your horse does not know which movement is coming next. Once you have a feel for how your horse reacts as he is going through the movements and transitions of the test, set up a miniature dressage arena in your living room, and practice by walking through the pattern of the test you will be performing. Put pieces of paper down where the various letters are so that you know which movement or transition is required at each letter. By doing this, you can practice your test more often than you can while mounted. It is probably better to do this while your family or significant other is out of the house, or you might get some very strange comments.

tip 41. Transitions

Practice being accurate with your movements and transitions. The lower-level dressage tests are basically walk-trot-canter tests, and all the horses in your division can do the paces. If your horse goes quietly, in a steady frame, and performs the required movement or transition at the correct letter, you will place well. The transition should occur when your boot is at the letter.

In order to become more accurate, go down the long side of an arena at the trot. Apply your normal aids as you pass a letter to bring your horse to the walk somewhere after the letter. Make a mental note of where you were along the side of the arena when your horse walked. Now turn back and measure how long it took you to achieve the transition from the application of your aids to the place where the transition occurred.

Once you have an idea of how long it takes for this transition to occur, mentally select a point that is the same distance before the letter, and practice the same transition again, but this time you should go from trot to walk very close to the letter. It may take a horse's length to make the transition at first, but remember that as your dressage improves, this distance between the application of the aids and the actual transition will shorten from a horse's length to one or two steps.

tip 42. Stiffness

Your horse probably has a stiff side. When you turn one direction it feels easy and smooth, yet when you turn the other direction you feel as if your rein is tied to a tree. Your immediate instinct will be to pull on the stiff side. Don't do that!

What we feel as stiffness on one side is actually the absence of feeling on the other side. In order for your horse to be stiff, he has to advance the shoulder on his stiff side and "spit out the bit" on the other side. Thus your job is not to pull against his stiff side, but to push your horse with one leg at the girth so that he brings his shoulders into alignment and picks up a connection with the soft rein.

For example, if your horse is stiff on the left, his body will be curved to the right, and he will be shorter on his right side than he is on his left, even when turning to the left. This is caused by a lack of elasticity in your horse's right side, and you must develop exercises that allow your horse to stretch his right side until he can pick up the bit.

tip 43. The Accelerator and the Brakes

During your dressage lessons, you will be continually reminded to ride from your inside leg to your outside hand. Why? Because when you are riding between your inside leg and outside hand, you are riding between the accelerator and the brakes. If you soften your outside rein and increase your inside leg, your horse should step smoothly forward. If you soften your inside leg and squeeze your outside hand, your horse should slow down.

It is simple; it is just not easy.

tip 44. Lateral Exercises

Teach your horse simple lateral exercises right away. If you do not know how to do a turn on the forehand or a leg-yield correctly, then learn how to do them. These and many other lateral exercises are your best tools to develop your horse's hindquarters and improve his flexibility; lateral work teaches your horse to step under his body with his hind legs in response to your leg aid. At first, I teach my horses to do simple lateral exercises (turn on the forehand and leg-yielding) along the wall of the arena. Your horse will keep his balance better if he has the support of the wall, and this will help you to make progress. Later on, I will ask for a turn on the forehand on the centerline, leg-yielding on the diagonal, and so on.

tip 45. Displacing the Shoulders

Once your horse has been introduced to lateral work, you want to have the feeling that whenever you are riding on a curve, you can displace your horse's shoulders to the outside of the curve. By this I mean that without losing the regularity or the bend, you can make the curve larger or smaller. This is an excellent exercise to make sure that your horse is responsive to your inside leg, and that you are riding from your inside leg to your outside hand. The exercise is deceptively simple, and will take some time and training before you can do it smoothly in both directions at all three paces. What you will find is that you will not be able to do it correctly unless you are using the correct aids.

Put your horse on a 20-meter circle at the trot to start this exercise. At first, it will help you to look down over your horse's outside shoulder. As your horse's outside front foot touches the ground, apply your inside leg at the girth in rhythm with the trot step. Make sure you do not close your outside leg or your horse will become confused. Each time you apply your leg, your horse should step under his body more with his inside hind leg, and should make the size of the curve a little larger. Have the feeling that each time you use your inside leg, you feel your horse reach for the outside contact. This exercise will not work if you use any other set of aids than the inside leg and the outside rein.

tip 46. Self-Carriage

All types of horses should be in self-carriage. Self-carriage means that the horse is not keeping his balance by leaning on your hands. I especially like eventers to be in self-carriage, because they must gallop and jump over uneven terrain.

As a simple check of your horse's self-carriage, put your horse on a mild curve at the walk, trot, or canter. (You should be able to do this exercise in any of the three paces, in either direction.) While on the curve, move your inside hand forward until a loop appears in your inside rein. Take special care that none of your other aids change and that you move only your inside elbow to soften the inside rein. If you lean forward from the shoulders or the hips, your horse will fall on his forehand and the value of the exercise will be lost. Leave the slight loop in the inside rein for several steps or strides, and then resume the contact. Make sure you pick up the same or slightly less contact than before. There should not be anything sudden or harsh about this movement, just a slight loss and regaining of the contact with the inside rein. If your horse is traveling in self-carriage, he will not change his step or stride, although you have softened the rein for a short period.

Your position must be stable and sensitive when you attempt this, as it is difficult to move only one rein at a time. If you soften your inside rein and maintain your outside rein and your horse stays the same, you are on the right track.

tip 47. Sit the Trot

The walk and the canter are relatively easy paces for you to sit, but the trot is another story altogether. Try this simple exercise to improve your ability to sit the trot: Look down your horse's shoulder, and imagine that you are pushing your seat bone down and forward into your horse's back in rhythm with your horse's front foot on that side. As his other front foot hits the ground, you should be pushing that seat bone down and forward. Experiment with your seat bones, until you have the feeling that you can elevate his trot by pressing more vigorously from side to side, and then can send him forward when you move your seat bones and add your legs at the girth.

Moving your seat bones in this rhythm will help you attach yourself to the motion of your horse's back at the trot. The trot is a difficult pace to sit because there is a lateral swaying motion of your horse's back as well as an up-and-down motion. When he pushes with one hind leg, his hip on that side drops down. At the same time, his opposite hind foot is coming underneath his body, which will cause his hip on that side to lift. Thus you are sitting on something that is going from side to side as well as back and forth. If you relax your hips into the exercise I just described, you will find the trot much easier to sit.

tip 48. Common Habits

Horses have common habits at the three paces, and you should have your corrections ready when your horse tries to develop a bad habit. For example, most horses will lose the rhythm of their walk, unless you keep an eye on them. Count your horse's steps silently, one-two-three-four, and then repeat. Make sure you have a steady, marching rhythm. If he stalls, use your whip behind your leg until he marches forward again. If he jigs or breaks into a canter, put him in a slight leg-yield, timing the action of your inside leg to the movement of his outside shoulder. Make him accept the action of your inside leg, and make sure you use your leg in the rhythm that you want. Do not quicken your leg aid as you apply it.

At the trot, your horse will have a tendency to either speed up or slow down. Very few horses maintain a regular trot without extensive training. Use the same basic approach you used for correction of the walk: if he stalls, use your whip, and if he quickens and rushes forward, put him into a mild lateral exercise until he accepts your inside leg.

Most horses will "canter like a dog," with their bodies curved around the rider's inside leg, even when going down the long side. To be straight down the long side, your horse must step in a straight line from his hock through his shoulder to his mouth on each side. Although we feel that his haunches have come inside the track, when your horse canters like a dog he has actually drifted with his outside shoulder. Tell yourself that you already have two out of the three points you need to be straight on the long side, because the hocks and the mouth are still in a straight line. Only the outside shoulder is out of alignment. Bring your outside leg forward to the girth, apply a slight outside indirect rein, and bring the shoulder into alignment. At first, this will only straighten your horse for a few strides, and then his shoulder will fall out again. Repetition will solve this over the long run. Cantering with the haunches inside the track is an interesting problem, because it is one of the few problems that cannot be solved by riding more forward.

tip 49. Build Your Skills By Showing

Go to local dressage shows to improve your dressage skills. You can ride several dressage tests in a day, and you do not have to worry about the other two phases. Best of all, you can have the tests read for you, which is a big advantage to your concentration. I also think it helps your horse to learn his job. If we are not careful, an event horse can come to believe that his role in life is to go down the centerline, misbehave, and then be rewarded for his misbehavior by being allowed to go galloping over jumps. Competing in several dressage tests in one day has the effect of teaching your horse to relax and concentrate during his tests.

tip 50. Even White Rats Learn from Experience

After each event, you can pick up your dressage-test score sheet at the secretary's office. Keep it, make a list of the comments from the judge, and improve those aspects before you compete again. Read your last few score sheets the night before your next event, and make a concerted effort to fix the comments. If you continually get comments like "reins too long" or "slumped in saddle," resolve to improve that part of your performance. You have been able to do it during your lessons with help from your trainer; now do it in the ring.

tip 51. Know the Difference

Learn the terminology for dressage. There is a big difference between a working trot and a medium trot, and the judge wants to see you display them both if they are part of the test. The USEF rule book contains descriptions of the various paces required and the definitions of the movements performed at each level. If you do not have any experience with dressage, read the rule book before you get too far into your learning process. When your instructor tells you that your horse is doing something that needs correction, you will at least know what the logic is for the adjustment you need to make.

Riders are not born knowing the difference between working trot and medium trot, so do not be surprised that it takes you a while to learn it. The correct medium trot will feel bigger to you, with more energy and bounce, and will probably be harder to sit. It will help to develop your feel if you watch videos of high-level dressage and go to local shows with high-level classes. Once you see the difference, you will have a much better idea of what your own horse should be doing when you ask for medium trot.

tip 52. Go Your Own Way

Each horse has a slightly different warm-up pattern before the dressage test. Some horses are better if worked for about forty-five minutes before the test, while others are better if you ride them twice. Some need a period of longeing, some are best if ridden for only a brief period, and so on. This is one of the many mysteries of horses, and you should view it as a challenge and a chance to get to know your horse, not as a source of exasperation. To make things even more complicated, your horse may change his warm-up pattern during the course of an eventing season. This is due to the additional fitness your horse gains as the season progresses. This will usually happen with a horse that starts out needing only a short period of warm-up, but becomes more tense in the arena from week to week. Experiment with different warm-up periods until you find the best new pattern. Make a mental note of it, as the pattern will probably repeat itself when you start your next season.

tip 53. Coordinate Your Schedule

Most horses are not quite as good in their dressage the day after jumping or cantering, so plan this into your schedule. If you have such a horse, plan on practicing your test movements the day before the jumping or cantering day, and devote the day after jumping or cantering to stretching and relaxation exercises. Make the training schedule work for you, not against you. If your horse is a trifle lazy, the best day for dressage may be the day after a canter, as he is energized and active after going determinedly forward the day before. This is one of the most satisfying aspects of training eventers, but you have to pay serious attention to your horse's reactions in order to gain the benefits of your knowledge.

III.

Cross Country

tip 54. Time Is of the Essence

Buy a stopwatch, and learn how to use it. You will need it to time your conditioning work. As you progress up the levels of eventing, time becomes an increasingly important part of the competition. More advanced events are won by fractions of a second, so develop good habits now. Wear your watch on hacks, or when riding your horse for pleasure. Practice starting and stopping your watch without looking down, until it becomes second nature. If you do this now, you won't have to learn a new skill when you graduate to the upper levels.

tip 55. Cross-Country Stirrup Length

At the Novice and Training levels of eventing, keep your stirrups the same length as your show-jumping length (see Tip 81). If you have your stirrups adjusted so that you have a 90-degree angle behind your knee, your stirrups are short enough for the speed you will be traveling at and for the height of the obstacles you will be jumping.

Once you start competing at the upper levels, you will be jumping larger obstacles at a faster rate of speed, so you will need a shorter stirrup. The shorter length will allow you to stay in balance with your horse, to keep more space between your seat bones and your horse's back, and to sit farther back when jumping larger drop fences. But not now.

tip 56. Ride Shorter at Home

Although I want you to compete with the same length of stirrups for cross country and show jumping, you should practice with your stirrups one or two holes shorter at home. However, you should not do this until you are confident about conditioning canters, and your horse easily maintains a steady pace throughout the conditioning period. Once you are sure of your situation, shorten your stirrups for the next conditioning day. You will be surprised at the increase in the physical workload that even one-hole-shorter stirrups will cause. Expect to be a little winded and to get a little tired, especially in your lower back. If this exercise affects you too much, just do the trot sets in shorter stirrups, and then let them back down for the cantering sets.

The benefits of this exercise are that you will dramatically improve your own fitness, you will become far more confident in your regular length of stirrups, and you will be preparing for the next level of competition.

tip 57. Conditioning Canters

Find a conditioning field where you can do your conditioning canters. The location should have consistently good footing, be mowed on a regular basis, and be more-or-less level. A slight rise and fall in the terrain is a good thing, but avoid steep hills and valleys. A local racehorse track is an acceptable substitute, if you can arrange to use it when the racehorses are not galloping on it. A racehorse going past you at 20 miles an hour can turn a normally placid horse into a raging maniac. This can be an upsetting experience for you and your horse, and might even prove dangerous.

tip 58. Horse Fitness

Learn how to get your horse fit. Many of the eventing books mentioned in the bibliography have chapters about conditioning, and some of them have sample schedules for conditioning horses for a specific level of competition. See Appendix 2 for sample conditioning schedules.

Proper conditioning takes time, but it is your greatest defense against an injury to your horse. Remember to start out slowly and patiently, introduce the canter preparation gradually, and avoid extreme speed whenever possible. Speed is probably the greatest cause of injury to the horse.

tip 59. Rider Fitness

Get yourself as fit as your horse. You will need to take some further form of exercise in order to deal with the rigors of galloping cross country. I have included some books in the bibliography. However, there are things you can do at the stables that will help you become stronger and fitter. Sweep the aisles with a broom, not a blower. Actually groom your horse, instead of just hosing him down after his ride. This will improve your horse as well as you.

If you have reached an important birthday milestone, say thirty, then spend a few minutes doing stretching exercises before you start riding for the day. Follow the stretching by "sitting on the wall." Put your back flat against a wall with a firm, smooth surface. Slide down the wall, keeping 90-degree angles

Sitting against the wall is an easy exercise to do, and requires no special equipment.

at your hips and knees. Now stay there as long as you can. That didn't take long, did it?

Work at this exercise until you can stay comfortably sitting against the wall for the amount of time that you will be out on course during your next event. This is a simple exercise, which is actually quite difficult, and is a good quick-check of your riding fitness level. It will not do much for your wind or your upper-body strength, but your back and legs will be ready.

tip 60. The Need for Speed

Practice riding at the correct pace for your level of competition. If you are going to a Novice event, you should know what 350 meters per minute feels like, both on the flat and over fences. Sooner or later you are going to have to buy a meter-measuring wheel, so go ahead and do it now. Take your new wheel up to your conditioning field and measure out several loops. Make one of the loops 350 meters long, then another 400 meters long, and a third loop 450 meters. Practice riding through these three loops at the required speed, using your stopwatch at first.

Later on, have a friend time you around the loop, while you concentrate on your feel rather than depending on your stopwatch. As a further training practice, do all three loops in sequence, but do the first loop at 350 meters per minute, the second loop at 400, and then the final loop at 450. Again, use your stopwatch at first, and then gradually train yourself to be able to go from one speed to another accurately without using your watch.

tip 61. Ride Shorter on a Puller

Many event horses take a keen interest in their work, and pull during conditioning sessions and competitions. It is counterintuitive at first, but the more your horse pulls, the shorter you need to ride in order to control him. It is easier to hold your horse when you can keep your hands at the level of his withers and put your weight lower in your hips and farther back behind the saddle. When riding with longer stirrups, the temptation to raise your hands, stand up, and put your weight directly against your horse is irresistible. Once you confront your horse's weight directly with your own, you will lose the struggle for control.

tip 62. The Pulley Rein

If you feel that your horse is getting out of control at the gallop, slow down and reestablish control by turning your horse into a gradual curve, and keep making the curve tighter until you are finally going in a circle at a comfortable speed again. Once this has occurred, open the size of the circle and continue your work.

To prevent your horse from seriously running away, learn how to use a *pulley rein*. The pulley rein can be used with either hand. Practice changing sides from time to time so that your horse does not become accustomed to it.

Take your left rein straight across the withers to the right side of the withers, and have the feeling you are pressing your left hand down toward the point of your right big toe. Your left hand should cross

Use the pulley rein when you need to slow down quickly. This is a harsh technique, and should only be used as a final resort.

under your right hand. At the same time, bring your right hand strongly up and back toward your right hip. You will probably feel your horse respond immediately, so remember to soften the reins as a reward. The pulley rein is an emergency aid, and has no place in the normal training of your horse.

tip 63. Uneven Terrain

You need to feel comfortable galloping over undulating terrain, but if you haven't done much cross-country riding, that may be easier to say than to do. Just as with everything else to do with horses, start out small and easy, and progress from there. If you have spent your entire riding career in a ring, then a simple hack outside with a more experienced companion will be enough of an adventure. Once you have adjusted to not having a fence to confine your activities, start to trot across uneven ground for short periods. Pick the most level part of the field. If your horse is at all fractious, by all means come back to the walk and try again after he has settled down.

After you are comfortable trotting up and down mild slopes, progress to the canter. Again, choose a more-or-less level area for your first few canter periods, and bring your horse back to the trot or walk if you are gaining too much speed. Gradually introduce steeper terrain as your control of your position and of your horse improves.

tip 64. Cross-Country Schooling

Any rider new to eventing needs to practice cross-country obstacles until she and her horse become comfortable with them. This especially includes banks, ditches, and water jumps. Locate a facility with good footing and a wide variety of schooling jumps that are suitable for your level.

Do not go out with the attitude that you are immediately going to jump the biggest obstacle you can find. Locate the smallest bank available, for example, and trot back and forth, up and down, until you are used to the sensation of landing one level higher or lower than your takeoff point. Later on, as your confidence level rises, you can make the bank more difficult by adding portable standards and rails.

Do the same thing with ditches; find a ditch that is so small and shallow that any horse will cross over it without difficulty. Once your horse is relaxed, move to a slightly wider ditch and repeat the process of trotting and cantering back and forth over it. It usually does not take much time before your horse is ready to jump simulated ditch-and-rails, Trakehners, and coffins, again by the process of using portable rails and standards to gradually introduce the questions that course designers typically ask.

Use the same process to introduce water obstacles to your horse to ensure that he is capable and confident through water.

tip 65. Bank On It

There is no position that is exactly perfect for you to use when going cross country, but there is a correct position for banks in particular. By this I mean that you should be much farther behind the motion jumping down a bank than when jumping back up the same bank from the other direction. Certainly you should always be a little bit behind the motion when jumping at speed. As your speed increases, your position has to become more defensive in order to ensure your stability and safety.

However, be aware of how much of an effort you need to make to be with your horse when jumping up larger banks. The slightest feeling that you are falling back in the saddle will cause your horse to catch his hind legs on the top of the bank. If you make a bad situation even worse by pulling on the reins to find your balance, your horse will "leave a leg" when jumping, and may even be injured in the process. Know when to sit with your horse's motion, and when to sit behind it. The best solution I have found for this is to trot up and down small banks on a loose rein, and practice adjusting your position according to whether you are jumping up or down.

tip 66. Two-Point and Light Three-Point Positions

There are two basic positions you will use when going cross country: two-point and light three-point. The two-point is also referred to as the galloping position. When you are in two-point, your weight is suspended entirely on your knees, with the feeling that your weight slips down into your ankles with every stride that your horse takes. Your seat bones should not touch your horse's back when you are in two-point. (Interestingly enough, the two-point is also the top of your posting motion, and is also the jumping position.) Practice your two-point. A lot.

The light three-point is used for the approach to the obstacle. A light three-point, also referred to as a half-seat, requires your seat bones to touch the saddle while your weight rests completely on the saddle. Because you are in jumping-length stirrups, your shoulders should be positioned more above your knees than above your hip bones. This position gives you more stability, which makes the application of your aids easier and more controlled.

Remember to make a smooth transition between two-point and light three-point. Do not suddenly bang down on your horse's back, or he will hate you forever.

tip 67. All You Need Is Balance

You do not need accuracy to jump cross-country obstacles success-fully—you need balance. When you consider that the horse high-jump world record is more than 8 feet, and you are jumping about 3 feet, you would agree that you have quite a margin for error. By now you have probably had the experience of jumping the same practice fence twice—once well and once badly. More than likely, the differ-ence between the two sensations was not *where* you jumped, but *how* you jumped. If you have a choice between an out-of-balance presentation that happens to accidentally step on the theoretically perfect takeoff spot or a perfectly balanced approach that finishes somewhere in the vicinity of the perfect spot, choose balance over accuracy every time.

tip 68. Consistent Pace

Good cross country includes making sure you land going the same speed you took off. This does not mean you should jump every cross-country obstacle at the same speed. A good cross-country course will require you to jump a few obstacles slower than the average speed of your level and then will allow you to jump a few obstacles faster than the required average if you want to "make the time."

You can check on this during your schooling sessions by counting in rhythm with your stride up to the obstacle, and then count the same number as you canter away from the obstacle. Make sure the rhythm is consistent. Your horse will usually pause for an instant when he lands after the obstacle, which will become a bad habit unless you train him to land at the same pace. Horses that want to accelerate after the landing should be restrained as they land. If you lose your own balance and allow your horse to speed up for a few strides, it will become increasingly difficult to get him back to the desired pace. Land thinking about what you are going to do next. Don't land thinking about what you just did.

tip 69. Ride the Turn

Never half-halt before an obstacle when it is preceded by a turn. Turns slow you down and balance your stride, and you should let the turn set your horse up for the obstacle rather than using your reins. Find a simple log or rolltop that you can practice over, and jump it a few times until you and your horse are relaxed. Find a point that is six or eight strides away from the obstacle (about 100 feet) and canter toward that point along a line that is parallel to the face of the obstacle. This imaginary point is where you will turn 90 degrees, and approach the obstacle in a straight line.

As you approach the turning point, change from a galloping position to a jumping position, look at the top of the obstacle, open your inside rein and put your outside leg back, and put your outside rein against your horse's neck. As your horse turns toward the obstacle, your aids will become straight again. The turn will have engaged and balanced your horse; now all you have to do is maintain your rhythm.

Once this feels easy, practice the turn from the opposite direction. Over time, move the imaginary turning point closer to the obstacle, and test your ability to turn and jump an obstacle that is closer to the turn. Another variation is to make the turns from an uphill or downhill approach. The obstacle may be the same, but the terrain will change how your horse feels. Practice this until you are accustomed to it.

tip 70. Get Your Reins Back

You need your reins to steer your horse. However, over drops and water jumps you may have to let the reins slip through your fingers, and then regain them. First of all, tie a knot in the end of the reins. This strengthens the reins at their weakest point, and gives you a place to start when you pick them up.

To shorten your reins, hold both reins in your whip hand. Place your other hand on top of your whip hand, point your fingers down

Put one hand on top of your whip hand, with your fingers between the reins.

Next, lift your other hand forward and up, while you pull the reins back with your whip hand. Now drop the knot, move your whip hand forward to the rein on that side, and away you go.

through the reins, and bring that hand up and back towards your shoulder. Practice this movement until you can do it with your eyes closed and with either hand. I recommend using your whip hand to hold the knot while you adjust the length of the reins with your other hand, because I feel it is easier to pick up the reins without controlling the whip at the same time, but this is merely a matter of choice.

tip 71. Ride Forward

If you are going to "miss" your distance, you always want to miss your distance going forward, not pulling back. First of all, distance is not too important when going cross country and your experience level is such that you should be concentrating on rhythm instead of accuracy anyway. If you get to an obstacle with a little too much impulsion, your horse can always use that impulsion to make his adjustment, and you will land safely on the other side.

If you miss your distance pulling on the reins, your horse can quite rightly say, "Heck, she obviously doesn't want to jump it, so why should I?" Most of the great cross-country riders I have ever known have been slight over-riders for just this reason. If you go forward and miss, your horse will forgive you. If you pull backward and miss, your horse will never forgive you. It is as simple as that.

tip 72. The Eyes Have It

Look where you want to go. This means both that your eyes should be focused on the imaginary path along which you and your horse will be galloping in the next few seconds, and that you should look at the top of the obstacle as you approach it. Although rider accuracy is not necessary to be successful cross country, looking at the jump tells you what sort of adjustment your horse needs to make in the last few strides in order to jump the obstacle well.

As you jump, it does not matter if your horse leaves a little long or gets a little close. What matters is that you and your horse move in harmony. If he is going to stand off, close your legs at the point of takeoff, and close your hip angle. If he is going to be a little close to the obstacle, keep your foot slightly in front of your knee while you keep your legs on, and make sure you do not jump ahead of your horse. If you and your horse do the same thing at the same time, it is not a mistake, it is an adjustment. Since you will need some form of adjustment every time you jump, concentrate on looking at the top of the fence. When you look at the obstacle you will be able to see what your horse is going to do, and what you can do to help.

tip 73. Cross-Country Attire

Cross-country attire should be distinctive without being distracting. Choose colors that are similar to the colors you have chosen for your stable colors, keeping in mind that hot pink is probably not the best of all possible choices. The purpose of your colors is to help identify you to your friends and family when you gallop into view, and secondarily to assist jump judges with identification when they are unable to see your number.

Resist the temptation to have matching everything, from your reins down to your bell boots. Anything your horse wears should be flat leather with no brass or color involved. Your saddle pad should be white, should fit your saddle, and should not be a billboard for various commercial entities. Remember that anything that draws attention away from your horse is not desirable.

For summertime competition, a solid-color polo shirt, matching helmet cover, tan britches, black boots, and brown or black gloves are always acceptable. When you are riding cross country, a protective vest is required. In colder weather you may substitute a long-sleeved turtleneck or a sweater in your stable colors. Your boots and spurs should sparkle the same way your horse's coat should gleam.

Make sure your helmet meets the safety standards required in the rule book. Once you have done this, make sure the helmet fits you correctly. If you think your helmet is slightly too tight, it is probably just right.

This rider is ready to step into the start box. Everything is neat and clean, and the overall picture is very attractive.

tip 74. Walk This Way

If at all possible, try to walk the cross-country course with a knowledgeable coach. Your coach can explain to you the problems presented by the various obstacles, and recommend a solution. The best test of a good cross-country coach is how closely his or her description of the course matches how it feels to you when you ride it. "Wow, she said that drop would feel like that. I am glad she told me to sit back, because I was in the air for a long time!"

tip 75. Fine-Tune Your Plan

When you are walking the cross-country course, occasionally look back along the track you have walked to this point. Often you will notice changes in the terrain and adjust your line accordingly. The same goes for turns—look back at the turn after you have walked through it. You will quite often change your mind a bit about where and when you are going to turn, once you see where you want to come out of the turn. The joke I tell on my course walks is that your horse should finish the cross-country course thinking, "Boy, this rider really knows what she is doing. It is almost as if she had walked the course!" My point is that the only thing you can really bring to the party is the knowledge of what is coming next. Your horse will develop such confidence in you that he will jump some very scary-looking obstacles knowing that you have done your homework.

tip 76. Walk It Again

Walk your cross-country course at least twice. The first time you walk, make sure you take a copy of the official map. This map is usually included in the competitor's packet that you will pick up when you arrive on the grounds. Use the map to orient yourself, to get an overall impression, and to make sure you follow the correct path for your course. You should not make any important decisions about how you are going to approach each obstacle the first time around. Save those decisions for later inspections.

tip 77. The Second Time Around

Most events have multiple levels of competition going on the same date, and this can be a bit confusing. Each level of competition (Novice, Training, and so on) will have a specific color for its obstacle numbers. This will be a big help to you as you walk around the course. The second time around the course should take you at least an hour, so allow enough time in your schedule for the day.

Take a pencil and paper, as you will want to make notes about the various decisions you will make during this inspection. These notes can include which side of a tree you plan to turn around, the location of any marginal footing, the options available at various combinations, and anything else that is important to remember about your course.

Having your coach walk around again with you is a great help, but it is not entirely necessary. If your coach is busy, take good notes about your plan, and go over them with the coach later.

tip 78. Combinations

Your cross-country course will probably contain several combinations. Review the rules for jumping combinations, so you know how to extricate yourself if you have a refusal at one of the elements. Walk the alternate approaches on one of your course walks, and then make a "plan B" so that you do not get flustered because you made one mistake, and make several more before negotiating the combination successfully. To a great extent, coolness under pressure is a result of careful preparation, so spend as much time as you can getting ready mentally as well as physically.

For example, you might plan to jump a ditch and go straight forward to an oxer. But if your horse is sticky over the ditch, you can pull off to the side, go around a tree, and jump a vertical. Plan A is the straight line, and plan B is the long way around the tree. Plan B takes longer, but it avoids the problem of having a sticky jump over the ditch and then getting to the oxer on a weak stride.

tip 79. Positive Visualization

Once you have made your plans for the cross-country course, sit down in a place where you can concentrate and make a video in your mind of the entire course. Make it as complete as possible. By this, I mean visualize your route from the stables to the warm-up area, how long you are going to warm up, then the route to the start box, what the first fence looks like, what your route to the second fence will be, and so on to the finish line.

This mental video should include any decisions you have made about where to turn before or after fences, what parts of the course have deep or hard footing, and any other special considerations. Don't forget to make a separate video for plan B's.

Stadium Jumping

tip 80. Show-Jumping Attire

Your attire for show jumping should be the same as for dressage, except that you will need a jumping helmet. Carry a whip, because it is impossible to go back to the trailer and get one when you discover that your horse has just developed a case of stage fright. Horse sports are about the horse, not about the rider, so avoid anything that calls attention to you rather than your horse. Don't forget your medical armband.

tip 81. Correct Stirrup Length

To adjust your stirrups correctly for show jumping, halt your horse. Have someone hold him if he is restive. Drop both of your feet out of the stirrups and let your legs hang straight down. Now adjust the stirrups so that they touch you at or just above your ankle bone. When you regain your stirrups, you will find that this adjustment has put approximately a 90-degree angle behind your knee. This is the correct length for jumps up to 3'6" and less than 400 meters per minute.

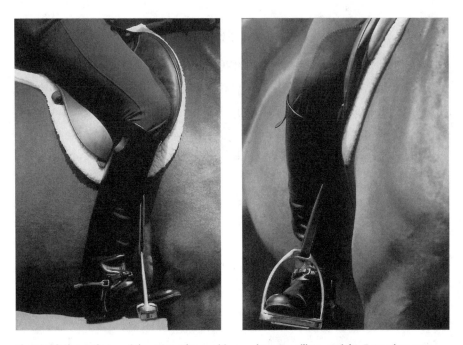

Sleep with these photos of the correct leg position under your pillow at night. Every time you place your foot into the stirrup, you should try to look like this. Note also the correct placement of the spur and the buckle on the strap; the spur is parallel to the seam on the heel of the rider's boot, and the buckle is exactly centered. Photo credit: Mandy Lorraine/*Practical Horseman*

tip 82. Stirrup Position

After you have adjusted your stirrups, pay careful attention to how you put your foot in the stirrup. Your stirrups are the ground for you while you are jumping, so you want to land in the correct place. Put the ball of your foot on the tread of the stirrup. Place your little toe against the outside branch of the stirrup, and angle the stirrup slightly across your foot. Now stand in the stirrups and press your heels down, then gently ease yourself back into the saddle. Allow your toes to turn out from your horse's body at the same angle with which you walk. You should be able to rise and sit without undue exertion.

Do not adopt any unnatural angle when riding. If it is not natural, it is forced, and anything forced in your riding will be stiff, and stiffness is the enemy of good horsemanship. Make sure the stirrup leather maintains a vertical line to the ground throughout the jumping effort. Once you have these relationships, keep them through constant work and repetition. You will develop a good leg the same way the concert violinist got to Carnegie Hall: "Practice, practice, practice."

tip 83. Martingales

Bill Steinkraus (1968 Olympic Individual Gold Medal winner in show jumping) once told me that my horse was not properly tacked up for jumping unless he was wearing a running martingale. I said that my horse did not toss his head. His reply was that a martingale that fits correctly does not act until you need it, and then you really need it.

To adjust the martingale correctly, imagine a horizontal line from your horse's hip through the point of rotation of his shoulder to his mouth. Your martingale should allow your horse to raise his head and neck until his mouth is just above this line, and then it should act. When jumping bigger drops cross country, let the martingale out one more hole, which will allow your horse the freedom to raise his head and neck when he lands over a bigger drop.

Make sure you have martingale stops on your reins. They prevent the rings on the martingale from catching on the bit. When the rings catch, your horse is very likely to panic, and may rear or even go over backwards. For the same reason, I never like to see a full-cheek snaffle used with a running martingale. There is a great risk that even with martingale stops, the ring may catch on the full-cheek and cause an accident. Also, make sure the buckle is centered between your horse's legs.

If your horse needs a breastplate as well as a martingale, consider using a polo breastplate with a leather loop sewn on the front. Take your martingale apart, so that all you have is the part with the rings and the buckle that passes over the girth. Thread the rings up through the loop on the breastplate, and you will have both requirements in one, without the extra strap that would otherwise be involved.

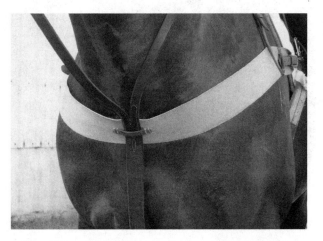

It will simplify your life if you only have one strap over your horse's neck during the jumping phases of an event.

Leather galloping boots with foam-rubber lining and tongue-in-buckle fasteners are ideal for jumping.

tip 84. Leg Protection

Horses are distressingly fragile creatures, for all their size and strength. I make it a practice to have some form of protection on their legs whenever they are doing any work. Polo bandages are usually sufficient for dressage work and hacking, while I prefer leather galloping boots for galloping, jumping, or cross-country schooling. If you are jumping or schooling in wet conditions or you are going to be practicing water jumps, don't use polo wraps, as the weight of the water will drag them down. An application of waterproofing paste on your leather galloping boots before you use them will make your cleaning process much simpler, and will help extend the life of a fairly expensive piece of equipment.

Shop around until you find leather galloping boots with foam-rubber lining. The boots should have tongue-in-buckle fasteners. Velcro closures or metal clips will open up under pressure, thus allowing the boots to slide down, and possibly injure a tendon. When you put the boots on, remember to have the buckles on the outside, with the straps pointing towards the rear.

tip 85. Breastplates

Use a breastplate when jumping and galloping. A breastplate keeps your saddle from sliding back, and can also serve as a martingale attachment. There are several types of breastplates, but the most useful are the hunting and polo breastplates (see illustration with Tip 83). My personal preference is the polo breastplate, because I feel it does the best job of keeping the saddle in place, and can also be used to hold a running martingale. This has the added advantage of having only one neck strap, rather than two. You should be able to put four fingers between your horse's chest and the breastplate. Make sure that any buckles will not chafe or pinch your horse, or cause an uncomfortable bump under your own leg.

The hunting breastplate does an acceptable job, but the saddle will slip more, and it is difficult to fit the running martingale correctly, as the attachment from the breastplate to the reins must be a different length for each horse. Just as with the running martingale, make sure the buckle between your horse's legs is centered so as not to cause a painful rub.

tip 86. Studs

I am often asked, "At what level should I start using studs in my horse's shoes?" I reply, "At what level do you want your horse to stop slipping?" The point is that we never want our horse to slip in the approach to a jump or on a turn, so we should always use studs (also referred to as caulks) when jumping on grass or uncertain footing. Make sure your farrier knows how to set your horse's shoes up to accept studs.

You will need a small toolbox to store your studs, tools, oil, various wrenches, and picks to maintain the studs in working order.

You need several sizes of studs so you will be ready for all types of footing. The studs shown here, from left to right, are suitable for firm, then medium, and finally deep footing.

Whenever you are not jumping, take the studs out. Leaving the studs in the shoes can make your horse footsore. When the studs are taken out, immediately replace them with blanks (studs that fill the stud holes but have no height). If you leave the holes open, they will become packed with dirt and gravel. The debris may damage the threads so that you cannot screw the studs in the next time you are riding on less-than-perfect footing.

tip 87. On the Contact, Not on the Bit

Your horse sees in focus wherever his nose is pointing. It is important to know this, because it determines the shape of your horse's frame in the approach to an obstacle. Bring your horse to the jump "on the contact" but not "on the bit." He should be allowed to poke his nose at the jump. Much of the disagreement that goes on between horse and rider in the approach to a jump starts with the horse raising his head and neck to look at the jump. The next time he does this, let your hand come higher above his withers the same amount that he raises his neck. Maintain the straight line from your elbow to your horse's mouth, and keep the same contact.

If your horse raises his neck quickly in the approach, you might fall back in the saddle, because the distance between you and your horse has shortened. Avoid this, as it will cause him to hollow his back and run against the bridle. Tell yourself that you need to let your hands float up with his mouth, and that your shoulders should stay above your knees. This does not mean that you should let your horse rush at the obstacle, as that is clearly undesirable. It means that you should not lean back onto your tailbone and close your heels in a vain attempt to keep your horse from rushing. Horses that rush in the approach usually need less leg and seat support, not more. If your horse tries to rush at his jumps, the sensation you should have is that you lessen the pressure of your seat bones while you increase the pressure of the reins.

tip 88. Learning to Pace Distances

Learn to pace distances accurately. Buy a 100-foot tape and measure out common distances that you will have to recognize when you walk the show-jumping course. Set out 12-foot, 24-foot, 36-foot, 48-foot, and 60-foot distances. These distances correspond to bounce, one, two, three, and four strides.

Put markers down so you know where the distance begins and ends. Pace back and forth between the two markers with 3-foot strides until your pace is absolutely accurate. For example, pace the 24-foot distance until you take exactly eight paces between the markers. Then move to the 36-foot distance, and so on. When you pace a distance, do not look at the next jump. Soften your eyes, look ahead, and just keep pacing until you get to the next jump. If you have stepped slightly under the next rail, or are still a foot or so away, then you know what the actual distance is, and how your horse will fit into it.

Practice this skill until you can pace 60 feet to within 6 inches of accuracy. Do not be surprised that you have to go back to the markers and recalibrate your pace every few months. This will be especially true if you have sprained your ankle or had some other riding injury. Accurate pacing may seem like a small detail, but consider that you are betting your life on the fact that you know the distance between two obstacles.

tip 89. The Rhythm Method

Accuracy of striding will be important over obstacles, but not yet. During your approach to an obstacle, concentrate on *how* you step to the jump, not *where* you step. To help find your rhythm, start counting out loud in the approach to a jump. Count up from "one" until you get to the takeoff spot. Try to start at least six strides away, so you have time to internalize the rhythm. As you get to the jump, listen to your voice. Make sure it does not increase in speed or volume. The reason rhythm is so important is that when you hear the rhythm, you hear the balance. If the rhythm is speeding up, your horse is falling on his forehand. If the rhythm is slowing down, your horse is falling behind your leg.

Once you maintain your rhythm in the approach easily, count in the approach until the takeoff, then say out loud "land" when your horse lands on the other side of the jump, and count the same number of strides as you depart from the jump. The strides before and after the fence should be the same. If you can do this on a regular basis, you are pretty good over fences.

tip 90. Eye Control for Stride Control

Look at the fence as you approach it. Look at the top rail of a vertical, the front rail of an oxer, and the back rail of a triple bar. Obviously, you should not look down in the air, so there must be some point where your eyes move to the next jump, or the next turn. Look between your horse's ears until the jump goes out of sight. At that instant your eyes should move to the next jump.

Watch other people's horses go to their jumps. The horse looks at the top rail of the jump. When you look at the top rail as well, you and your horse are thinking about the same thing at the same time. Thus you will know if you are going to stand off at the jump a little bit or get there a bit close. These minor variations in your horse's takeoff point are not as important as the harmony between you and your horse. If you and your horse do the same thing at the same time, that is not a mistake, it is an adjustment.

tip 91. Practice Courses at Home

Practice at home things you know you will have to do during your show-jumping round. You can be sure you will have to jump an in-and-out, so practice it at home. As you practice them, analyze your horse's response. Is he jumping in too weakly and is unable to get out of a two-stride combination without chipping in a third stride? Does he invariably run out of room at the last obstacle in a combination because he jumps with such a flat arc? All these mistakes are normal training problems; develop a plan to train your horse so that they are no longer problems.

For example, if your horse consistently runs out of room at the end of an in-and-out, practice jumping and pulling up. Running through the distance means your horse is running through your half-halt, so you have to practice a full halt first. Once your horse gets the idea, you should be able to make the distance more comfortably.

tip 92. Turn, Turn, Turn

A good show-jumping course will ask you to turn both directions, so set up exercises during your lessons and practice sessions that simulate these turns. Invariably, one way will be more difficult for you than the other. View this as an opportunity to improve, and not as a problem. Devise ways to separate the problem into smaller pieces, teach the small pieces to your horse, and then put them back together again. If you cannot turn easily between two obstacles set 60 feet apart at 90 degrees to each other, then teach your horse to canter on a 20-meter circle, then a 15-meter circle, and finally a 10-meter circle. Obviously, your dressage has to improve for you to be able to turn more easily, but you need to practice turning over obstacles as well.

When you decide to improve your ability to turn, start with this simple exercise: Put a small (2' to 2'6") obstacle up in the center of the arena. Trot to it, and as your horse takes off, press your new outside leg back, open your inside rein, use a little neck rein, look in the direction you want to turn toward, and land over your new inside knee. After a little practice, your horse will start to land on the lead that you select as you leave the ground. Make sure to practice turning both directions.

Once you have the basics of turning, you just have to refine them, and practice tighter turns over larger obstacles at higher speeds. Remember that you turn your horse by going with the motion and using your outside leg and rein, not by leaning back and pulling on the inside rein.

tip 93. Liverpools

Introduce liverpools the same way you have done everything else—simply and easily. Buy a 12-by-12-foot tarpaulin, preferably bright blue in color. Lay it down between two standards, and fold it over on itself until it is barely wider than a rail. Put two rails down on the ground, one on either side. At this point, the question is more like a ditch than a liverpool. If your horse is spooky, ask a rider friend to give you a lead over it before attempting it on your own.

Once your horse jumps this "ditch" in a calm and sensible manner, you can unfold the tarpaulin slightly to increase the spread. Do this until he will step over a liverpool that is about three feet wide. Fold the tarpaulin back over to decrease the spread, and add some height to the back rail. Practice this until your horse is confident.

Now you can raise the front rail, and make an oxer liverpool. Change the spread or increase the height, but don't do both at the same time. Some horses understand this question right away, but some are spooky about it. Let each horse learn at his own pace. If yours needs a few extra sessions to be confident about liverpools, just think of it as an opportunity to have some fun with your horse.

tip 94. Training Sequences

You can simulate many of your cross-country questions in your show-jumping practice sessions, especially accuracy and straightness questions. Throughout these training sequences, keep in mind that you can make things higher for your horse, or you can make them more technical, but you should not increase both at the same time. When you introduce your horse to straightness questions, teach him to jump angled rails first. He should be equally comfortable jumping from a right-to-left or a left-to-right angle. Once he can jump one obstacle at 45 degrees, lessen the angle and introduce a second obstacle on the same angle. When you add the second obstacle, lower the height of both obstacles so that your horse does not feel overwhelmed.

One of my favorite straightness exercises is called the "to-and-fro rails." It will teach you to hold a line between angled rails and will also prepare you and your horse to jump a corner. Set up three jumps so that the distance between the standards is 28 feet and then 38 feet on one side, while the distance on the other side is the reverse— 38 feet and then 28 feet. (See the photo.) This will provide a two-stride distance if you are straight down the center of this exercise.

However, if your horse "fades" to one side or another while jumping, you will get to the next obstacle on a half-stride, which is an uncomfortable experience. Try it again, and keep your horse straight. Think to yourself that your line is straight, while the jumps are crooked.

Three jumps set up for the "to-and-fro rails" exercise.

tip 95. What's Your Angle?

Course designers these days are frequently asking Novice and Training horses to jump obstacles at slight angles. If you are going to meet the problem in a competition, you need to practice jumping at an angle to the face of the obstacle at home first.

Put two rails down in front of the obstacle to form a chute. Make sure they are perpendicular to the obstacle's top rail and that they are the same distance apart at both ends. Jump back and forth over the obstacle until your horse has accepted the two ground rails. Now pick up the far end of each rail and move it to the side one foot. Move both ends the same way. Now the ground rails still form a chute, but the chute forms a very slight angle to the obstacle. Again, jump back and forth over this until you and your horse are comfortable with the problem. Then move the ground rails another foot to the side. If you are successful with this additional angle, you have practiced it enough for one session.

In succeeding sessions, you can bring the chute to a 45-degree angle. Once you and your horse can handle it, take one of the ground poles away, replace the other ground rail at a 90-degree angle to the obstacle, and give your horse a refresher session in jumping at angles. This time you only have one ground rail as a guide, so you are increasingly on your own to maintain your straightness. Repeat the process of moving the end of the ground rail, until you can jump the obstacle at the same angle as you did when you still had a chute. Finally, go through the same process without the ground rail. If this poses no problem for your horse, you can graduate to jumping an offset in-and-out, and then finally the to-and-fro rails as shown in the illustration for Tip 94.

The ground poles should be perpendicular to the obstacle at first, and then moved off at an angle as you and your horse's confidence increases. As shown, the rails are set up for a left-to-right angle.

tip 96. Jumping Corners

Corners are easy to build in the show-jumping arena. Start your horse over a small oxer. Raise the oxer gradually until it is the height of your competitive level. Now lower it again, take away one standard, and place one rail on top of the other at the side with the single standard. To make sure your horse can see the back rail, raise the back cup by three inches on the two-standard side. The spread at the two-standard end should be half the size as when it was an oxer. You are now jumping a round oxer that is narrow at one end, so only jump it towards the slightly higher rail, or it would become an oxer with a false shape.

Now go through the same process as any other time you have introduced a new problem: explain it to your horse in a low, simple manner, and then gradually increase the difficulty. Each time I raise the corner, I narrow the spread, and each time I increase the spread, I lower the height.

To maintain your alignment over the corner, imagine a third rail that is higher than either of the two rails that form the corner. Mentally place this third rail between the two rails so that it bisects the angle formed by the top rails. Approach the corner on a line that would place you perpendicular to this imaginary rail. Doing this will put you at a slight angle to the front rail of the corner, and at the reverse angle to the back rail. This mental exercise will help you "split the difference" when trying to find your line to a corner.

Setting up a practice corner in your jumping arena is simple. All you need are three standards and rails arranged as shown here.

tip 97. Narrow Fences

Train your horse to jump through narrow openings the same way you train him to do anything else that you want him to do, calmly and easily. Start with the problem in miniature, explain it to him, let him learn it, and then progressively make the problem harder for him.

Build a small jump with 12-foot rails that your horse has seen before and that he jumps well. Let him canter back and forth over it until he is a bit bored with the whole thing. Place a post standard

Always make the question low and easy for your horse. Once he understands the question, you can make the opening much smaller.

with no cups attached just inside the jump standard on each side. As a safety factor, put the post standards on opposite sides of the rail. That way, if your horse hits the rail, it won't feel like a permanently fixed rail to him.

Notice that the extra standards are set on opposite sides of the rail, and they are at least the width of the pole away from it. This way, there is room for the rail to fall out of the cup should your horse make a mistake and hit the rail.

Chances are that your horse will not react to the post standards. If that is the case, bring each post standard in by 1-foot increments, which will narrow the opening by 2 feet. Make sure he is relaxed about this before you narrow the opening any more. If you do this twice, you will be cantering back and forth through an 8-foot opening.

During subsequent lessons you can gradually work the opening in until it is a minimum of 4 feet wide. After the opening gets down to 6 feet, you might lower the rail when you try the new smaller opening, to reassure your horse. I never ask my horses to jump anything narrower than 4 feet; if they will hold their line there, they would jump a sword stuck in the ground if you asked them to.

tip 98. Bad Boys!

Sooner or later your horse will refuse or run out at an obstacle, and you must have the correction ready for him. Run-outs and refusals are basically disobediences to your leg, and must be dealt with that way. For example, if your horse runs out to the left, stop him, bring him immediately back to the center of the obstacle (without circling or turning beyond the obstacle), punish him with your whip behind your left leg, turn to the right, and approach the obstacle again. Once he jumps it, pat him and praise him verbally so that he starts to understand right from wrong. It may seem unfair to you, but you must punish him for refusing even though you know you were part of the problem.

The hard truth is that a horse must jump, whether the situation is perfect or not. If you take the attitude that "it's all my fault, so I can't punish him," then the next time your horse gets to the jump a little wrong he'll say, "Oh, I couldn't jump, it wasn't perfect." You will never be able to learn to ride well over jumps without making mistakes, so train your horse that you will do everything you can, but when you get to the point of takeoff, he has to bail you out from whatever situation you have gotten the two of you into, whether the distance is perfect or not.

tip 99. Course Walk

When you get to an event and walk the show-jumping course, walk it with your horse in mind. If everyone is buzzing about the long distance in the last line, and you are riding a 17-hand Thoroughbred,

Walk your show-jumping and cross-country courses with your coach.

then you are all smiles. Likewise, a tight combination would suit a small, pony-gaited horse. Not every question on the course is a problem for your horse, so analyze the course with that in mind. In a good course, about one-third of the course will suit your horse, one-third will be of average difficulty for your level, and one-third will be hard for you and your horse to handle. If the time allowed is tight, save time by making economical turns, not by galloping faster.

Just as with the cross-country course, walk the show-jumping course at least twice, once with your trainer or a more experienced, friendly competitor, and then once on your own.

tip 100. Watch the Course

Watch a few horses go around your course, if you can. Note whether the time allowed is easy to make, or whether you will have to hurry to avoid time faults. Is that line better for your horse in four or five strides? Are the turns slippery, or hard to make? If there is a jump immediately after a turn, and you have a chance to watch a couple of horses go, then you should know how to get to the fence correctly. If all the horses got to the jump out of the turn on a half-stride, then you know what to do to make a nice effort there.

Remember to watch with your horse in mind. People may be struggling to make the distance out of a line, but if you have a horse with a naturally long stride, you should have no problem. Just because other horses are having problems with a part of the course does not necessarily mean you will too. Ask yourself whether the distances and obstacles are hard for *your* horse, not whether other people have been having problems with them.

tip 101. Warming Up

When you go to the warm-up ring for show jumping, warm up your horse with the idea of rehearsing the course you are going to jump in the competition arena. If the course is twisty and trappy, practice rollback turns to obstacles. If there is a wide oxer early in the course and the course is open and galloping, then practice a few maximum oxers from a stronger pace than usual. Your horse should feel that the course is an extension of the things you have already been doing in the warm-up arena.

Bonus tip: Enjoy!

Go out and smell the roses. Eventing is a hard sport to learn and become proficient at, and you need a good work ethic to improve. At the same time, you are involved with horses because you love them, so occasionally drop everything on a nice day, and go for a hack in the fields and woods. You and your horse will be the better for it tomorrow, and you will have an increased awareness of how lucky you are that you chose this sport. Good luck.

Grooming

Buy a small grooming kit, and keep it well stocked and clean. At a bare minimum, your kit should contain a curry comb or curry mitt, body brush with soft bristles, dandy brush with stiff bristles (never use the dandy brush above the knees because it is too stiff for your horse's skin), mane comb, hoof pick, hoof dressing, fly spray for summertime, antiseptic salve for minor wounds, and a clean rub rag.

Stand your horse in cross-ties in a clean, level, well-lit place. Pick out his feet, sweep the dirt off to the side, and dispose of it. Start the grooming process on his near side with the curry comb in your left hand and the dandy brush in your right. Place the curry comb behind your horse's ear, and use circular strokes to dislodge dirt, dander, and dead hair. When you use the curry comb, press your weight into it. You are trying to reach into your horse's pores and dislodge any dirt that might be in there. Every ten circles draw the dandy brush across the curry comb to strip out any dirt that the curry comb has picked up. Continue this action along your horse's body until you have reached the left hind leg. Switch sides, change the curry comb and dandy brush into opposite hands, and work your way down your horse's off-side. By the time you have finished this part of the process, you will be a little arm weary.

Take a deep breath, move back to the near side, put the body brush in your left hand and the dandy brush in your right, and start drawing the body brush down his neck, starting behind the left ear. Again clean the body brush with the dandy brush every ten strokes. While you used a circular motion with the curry comb, you should only work with the grain of the hair when using the body brush.

Put your shoulder into the grooming stroke with the body brush. You should feel that you are mildly thumping your horse when you start the stroke with the body brush. The intensity of the stroke should vary according to the location on your horse's body. You can press harder on his neck and hips than you can over his loins. This causes blood to rise to your horse's skin and improves his circulatory system. It also produces healthy skin oils.

Use the body brush all the way down to the cornet band on all four legs, and then take another deep breath. You will need it, as by this time your arms will feel as if you have been working out with Muhammad Ali. Your horse is not the only one who will benefit from daily grooming; your upper body strength will improve markedly after a month of daily exercise like this. Stand in front of your horse, and carefully use the curry comb on your horse's head. Repeat the process with the body brush, remembering to clean the body brush with the dandy brush on a regular basis.

Move to your horse's hind end, stand to one side, and gently comb out his tail with the mane comb. Any tangles should be picked out by hand. If you are pulling out tail hairs, you are going too fast and using too much force. A well-groomed horse has a full, clean, healthy tail that you can put your fingers into at the top and pull straight down without meeting any resistance or tangle. This will take some time with most horses, so work on this gradually.

During this process, you should have become aware of any minor cuts or scrapes and applied some antiseptic salve to the affected areas. Finish the job for the day with a coating of hoof dressing, and wipe your horse down with a clean rub rag before returning him to his stall. Remember to sweep the grooming area. A good horsewoman or horseman always leaves things cleaner and neater than he or she found them.

Shampoo gets dirt out of your horse's coat, but it is not "grooming." Grooming is the application of your very own elbow grease, applied liberally every day. A good horseman can instantly tell the difference between horses that are clean and horses that are well groomed. A horse that is being groomed daily will have a "bloom" on his coat that no amount of shampoo, additives, or cream rinse will supply. By a bloom, I mean the bronze tint that your horse's coat will show in direct sunlight. It is easier to see a bloom on bays and browns, but palominos and grays get a bloom as well.

If you are diligent in this process, I guarantee that in thirty days you will have a new horse on your hands. Your horse will be healthier and you will be fitter, and those are both good things.

Conditioning

Conditioning is your most important responsibility when it comes to your horse. You have a complex job ahead of you as you prepare for the three disciplines that make up an event, and conditioning will be your horse's best defense against injury. However, if you concentrate solely on his physical condition, you will produce a horse that is fit, but not fit to compete. So you have to make sure your horse is ready to compete in all of the phases. Think of yourself as a juggler who has to keep four balls in the air at one time. One ball represents your horse's physical fitness, another is his dressage, a third is his show jumping, and the fourth is his cross-country jumping. To be properly prepared for an event, you must take care of all four.

I train event horses using what I refer to as a "rotation." By this I mean that you must rotate through the four parts just described. How are you to do this? Well, remember that training your horse is an art, not a science. So there are many ways to prepare your horse; what you read here should be regarded as *an* answer, and not *the* answer. In fact, I will give you a couple of different rotations that you can use. Each rotation will work, but you should not switch back and forth between them without taking some time off from competing. This will allow your horse to adjust mentally and physically to the demands of the new rotation.

Any rotation should be a long-term program, should be progressive in its demands, and should be aimed at producing your horse at a certain level of fitness—not a continually increasing level of fitness. Particularly at the lower levels, it is equally as possible to produce your horse too fit as it is to produce him unfit. If you compete regularly, you will notice that your horse is getting fitter even though you are not increasing the amount of work that you are giving him at home. This is because the cross-country courses that you gallop over will have the effect of another gallop in your schedule. Horses hold their breath while they jump, which makes the act of jumping an anaerobic exercise, and judicious anaerobic exercise makes the horse fitter.

I think the interplay of the various parts of training is one of the more interesting aspects of training an event horse. You are training the whole horse for the whole event and not concentrating on one part of that event. Keep this in mind as you apply your rotation. Too much dressage and not enough jumping is not the correct approach, but too much jumping and not enough dressage is not the correct answer either.

I train most of my event horses using the following four-day rotation:

> Day 1—dressage
> Day 2—show jumping
> Day 3—dressage
> Day 4—conditioning work
> Day 5—repeat Day 1

The most physically stressful day in the rotation is Day 4. Therefore, the following day should be the easiest day. During the work period of Day 1, I tend to concentrate on stretching and suppling exercises. If my horse is a racetrack reject, I will probably have to concentrate on calming him. Long, low, and slow is the answer for that type of horse. If my horse is lazy, I will carry a dressage whip and make sure he is in front of my leg.

Day 2 is obvious, but note that you need to plan ahead if you are taking dressage or show-jumping lessons. Make sure the lesson occurs on the correct day in the rotation.

On Day 3 I tend to practice the dressage movements required at my competitive level. I will practice parts of the dressage test but I do not run through the test in its entirety, as my horse will soon learn the pattern and start to anticipate the movements.

On Day 4 I will usually warm up my horse at the trot and then do "sets" or periods of slow canter work. These sets should be planned out over a long period of time. Basically, your horse is fit enough to compete if he can slow canter twice the distance of his cross-country course. Remember to gradually increase your horse's workload. Do not come out tomorrow and slow canter three miles, or you may injure your horse.

Like most trainers, I use the interval system to get my horse fit. Horsemen have found that horses can tolerate exercise better if it is broken up into shorter periods, followed by a brief period of rest at the walk, and then another period of exercise, and so on. I describe the amount of work I am going to give my horse using what I call "interval notation."

For example, if I were going to warm up my horse for a total of fifteen minutes and then slow canter him for a total of twelve, I would write it down like this:

5" x 3 @ 220 w/ 2"i+
4" x 3 @ 400 w/2"i

This should be read as "for five minutes trot [220 meters per minute is the speed of the trot], then walk for two minutes, then trot for five minutes, then walk for two, then trot a final set of five minutes." Then you should walk for two minutes, and begin your cantering work. The notation described above would then continue "for four minutes slow canter [400 meters per minute is a brisk show-jumping pace], then walk for two minutes, then canter another four-minute set, walk for two minutes, and canter a final set of four minutes." I call this my maintenance work because it will maintain a good level of fitness for most Novice and Training horses. I would not increase this amount of work until I am ready to move to Preliminary.

When you complete the work described above, you will have covered about two miles at the trot and three miles at the canter. Remember to build your horse up to this level. If your horse is working in dressage for thirty to forty-five minutes a day, and can easily go through a thirty- to forty-five-minute show-jumping session, then he is fit enough to begin systematic conditioning work. For example, over a period of six times through the four-day rotation, your conditioning work would look like this:

Day 4–5" x 2 @ 220 w/2"i+
2" x 2 @ 350 w/2"i

Day 8–4" x 3 @ 220 w/2"i+
2" x 3 @ 350 w/2"i

Day 12–5" x 3 @ 220 w/2"i+
3" x 3 @ 350 w/2"i

Day 16–5" x 3 @ 220 w/2"i+
3" x 3 @ 400 w/2"i

Day 20–5" x 3 @ 220 w/2"i+
3" x 3 @ 400 w/2"i

Day 24–5" x 3 @ 220 w/2"i+
4" x 3 @ 400 w/2"i

Once your horse has been built up to this level, he should be fit enough to go for a cross-country school and shortly after to a local event. I tend to keep my horse in regular work, without a scheduled day off. After an event or a cross-country school, I would then plan to give my horse a day off.

When planning your rotation, work backwards from the event you hope to attend. Your next-to-last conditioning work should be eight days before the cross-country phase at your intended event, and the last work four days before. Once you have determined the days for your conditioning work, you can then plan your lessons in dressage and show jumping.

While it is important to work your horse on a regular basis, the above rotation is not the only one available. If you have a steady job and a family, you have to balance your family life with your horse life. To do this, it helps to have a day off from riding every week. Many of my students are in this situation, and their rotation looks like this:

Monday—hacking and/or hill work
Tuesday—dressage stretching and suppling
Wednesday—dressage movements
Thursday—show jumping
Friday—dressage
Saturday—conditioning
Sunday—day off

If you are just getting started in eventing, then you might need more practice in jumping, and your training rotation could look like this:

Monday—hacking and/or hill work
Tuesday—show jumping
Wednesday—dressage
Thursday—show jumping
Friday—dressage movements

Saturday—conditioning work
Sunday—day off

If your horse is getting on in years, or he is a little suspect in the soundness department, then your rotation might look like this:

Day 1—dressage stretching and suppling
Day 2—show jumping
Day 3—dressage movements
Day 4—conditioning work
Day 5—walk one hour or turn out
Day 6—repeat Day 1

Using this rotation allows your horse an extra day to recover from the exertions of the conditioning day, and it gives you the chance to give him a day off on a regular basis.

In all the above rotations, you should notice that there is a continual variety in the work you plan for your horse. I think horses enjoy variety. They come out of their stall excited and wondering about what they are going to do today. Once you have made your training plan, you should begin to keep an exercise diary. The schedule is what you plan to do, while the diary reflects what actually happened. The schedule might say "dressage," while your diary might say "shoe off, farrier late."

Keep your diaries from past training cycles. After several training cycles, you will notice patterns in your horse's reactions and in your competitive results. For example, you might notice that as the season progresses, your dressage scores get worse. One cause of this can be that your horse is getting too fit for his competitive level. Think about adjusting his schedule so that you skip a conditioning canter every now and then and substitute a dressage session.

Make sure that you use the schedule to train your horse. Don't let the schedule train you. If you are not doing well in one of the three phases, you need to adjust the schedule to compensate for it. Of all the challenges you will face while you are eventing, the continual adjustment of your horse's training cycle is the biggest. If you can consistently produce your horse ready to do well in all three phases, then you can truly call yourself a good horseman.

Bibliography

SUGGESTED INTRODUCTORY READING

Kane, Jeanne, and Lisa Waltman. *The Event Groom's Handbook*. Event Books International, 1983.

O'Connor, Sally. *Practical Eventing*. Half Halt Press, 1998.

Phillips, Mark. *Mark Phillips on Riding: A Complete Guide for Beginners*. Prentice Hall Press, 1986.

Shiers, Jessie. *101 Hunter/Jumper Tips*. Lyons Press, 2005.

United States Equestrian Federation (USEF) Rule Book.

Wofford, James C. *Training the Three-Day Event Horse and Rider*. Doubleday, 1995.

FITNESS

Midkiff, Mary. *Fitness, Performance, and the Female Equestrian*. Howell Book House, 1996.

Steiner, Betsy. *Equilates*. Trafalgar Square Publishing, 2003.

DRESSAGE

Decarpentry, General. *Academic Equitation*. Trafalgar Square Publishing, 2001.

German Equestrian Federation. *Advanced Handbook of Riding Techniques*. Half Halt Press, 1987.

——. *The Handbook of Riding Techniques*. Half Halt Press, 1987.

Lundquist, Bengt. *Practical Dressage Manual*. Published by the author, 1976.

Museler, Wilhelm. *Riding Logic*. Methuen & Co. Ltd., 1949.

CROSS COUNTRY

Fox-Pitt, William. *Schooling for Success*. David and Charles Ltd., 2004.

Green, Lucinda. *Cross-Country Riding*. Pelham Books Ltd., 1986.

Tait, Blyth. *Blyth Tait's Cross-Country Clinic*. Addington Ltd., 1999.

Wofford, James C. *Gymnastics: Systematic Training of the Jumping Horse*. Compass Press, 2001.

SHOW JUMPING

Chamberlin, Col. Harry D. *Riding and Schooling*. Derrydale, 1934.

——. *Training Hunters, Jumpers, and Hacks*. Derrydale, 1937.

Chapot, Frank. *Winning with Frank Chapot*. Breakthrough Publications, 1992.

de Nemethy, Bertalan. *The de Nemethy Method*. Doubleday, 1988.

Kursinski, Ann. *Ann Kursinski's Riding and Jumping Clinic*. Doubleday, 1995.

Morris, George. *Hunter Seat Equitation*. Doubleday, 1971.

Paalman, Anthony J. A. *Training Showjumpers*. Allen & Co. Ltd., 1998.

Pollmann-Schweckhorst, Elmar. *Training the Modern Show Jumper*. Trafalgar Square Publishing, 2005.

Steinkraus, William C. *Reflections on Riding and Jumping*. Doubleday, 1991.

——. *Riding and Jumping*. Doubleday, 1961.